# Eclectic Essays,

# Poems, Prose & Quotes

## By a Hopeful Human

# R.H.W. DORSEY

## Second Acts Press

All rights reserved. No part of this publication may be reproduced, distributed, or transmitted in any form or by any means, including photocopying, recording, or other electronic or mechanical methods, now known or unknown, without the prior written permission of the author and or publisher, except in the case of brief quotations embodied in critical reviews and specific other noncommercial uses permitted by copyright law.

This collection includes the author's new and previously published works.

©2024 R. H. W. Dorsey

Published by Second Acts Press, LLC

www.secondactspress.com

First print edition: 2024

IngramSpark Print ISBN: 979-8-3303-6126-7

Contact the author email: admin@rhwdorsey.com

# Dedication

*To my muse,*

*I am offering this to you because intangible thoughts sometimes need to be put to paper.*

## Table of Contents

Introduction ........................................................................................... 1
ESSAYS .................................................................................................. 3
   On Being a Grateful Soul ................................................................ 4
   Thoughts on Racism in America from a Hopeful Human ................ 10
   Being a Better Human – What's so Difficult? ................................. 19
   Perspective ..................................................................................... 23
POETRY & PROSE ............................................................................... 25
   Never ............................................................................................. 26
   Hello, Juneteenth! ......................................................................... 28
   Forever Blue .................................................................................. 31
   Love ............................................................................................... 32
QUOTES ............................................................................................... 33
ESSAY ................................................................................................... 37
     Justification ............................................................................... 38
     On Miracles ............................................................................... 40
     On Grief ..................................................................................... 45
POETRY & PROSE ............................................................................... 49
   Apathy Siege ................................................................................. 50
   You Chose Violence ...................................................................... 51
   Hate Exists .................................................................................... 53
QUOTES ............................................................................................... 55
End Notes ............................................................................................. 58

# Introduction

I first realized how much I enjoyed writing essays, poems, and prose as a teenager. My initial appreciation for writing back then was due to one reason—my thoughts on paper were more fluent than when I spoke the words out loud.

The following collection of poems, essays, and prose includes both published and previously unpublished content. Some of the included essays were written in response to current events in the news, while others were simply about topics that piqued my interest.

The first essay, *On Being a Grateful Soul,* was put on a shortlist of essays by Fountain Magazine in 2018 for the publication's contest. I was grateful for the acknowledgment.[1]

# ESSAYS

# On Being a Grateful Soul

I believe gratitude is learned and not inherent in human beings at birth. A newborn probably feels the love projected by its parents. Babies grow into children who observe interactions with the people surrounding them. As a child grows into a young adult, the individual choices they make are a result of their experiences. Adults who behave gratefully become the individuals they are because of their upbringing. Grateful people, I suppose, attain their characteristics through the process of life experience.

When I consider the subject of gratitude, one of my earliest memories stems from childhood. A dear aunt of mine was very attentive to me and opened my eyes to all the possibilities that learning could offer. My first visit to a public library was facilitated by my aunt when I was in elementary school. I recall walking into the building as she held my small hand. The librarian typed my name and other pertinent information on the wallet-sized cardboard. I have a vivid memory of being handed the light-orange colored card that meant *I* could choose a book and take it home. The children's section of the library on that day was filled with colorful tables and chairs. Some picture books were displayed upright on the small tables with chairs requiring no adult's help for me to sit. Other books were on the shelves, just waiting for me to choose. The attentive librarian asked me questions about the kind of books I liked. Being young and so overwhelmed by this experience, I had no answer for the librarian. She gave suggestions on several books, but I couldn't choose from the multitude of books tucked neatly in place on the surrounding walls. The selection of books was overwhelming for me as a young child. With direction from my aunt, I selected the books *Madeline by* Ludwig Bemelmans and *Curious George* by H. A. Rey & Margaret Rey. Walking to the desk to check out my first two library books is still fresh in my mind. The friendly librarian's face is long gone from my memory, but how she treated a shy little girl was not forgotten. I felt special that day. That first day at the library would become the first of many visits to the library with my aunt. The foundation of that early event began my love for books and, subsequently, writing. I'm eternally grateful to my aunt for spending time with me that day and more days than I can count since that time. The experience at the library was a single event that gave me a feeling of gratefulness. However, my mind now explores the question of why I was grateful for my experience on that day. I had no idea at the time I'd grow to love reading books and eventually writing. The answer lies in my experiences to that point in my young life. What was it about my experiences being introduced to books I now revere? Being a middle child in a family of eight children was my reality. I realized even back then, a gift was being presented to me. Why was it so special? It was a simple act of traveling to the library with a relative on the surface. The reason was I, unlike my brothers and sisters, benefited from the experience, and they didn't. I had a library card and was able to circulate books. I realized at the time I was given special treatment and felt sad that my siblings weren't given the same opportunity. In fact, I was given many opportunities throughout my childhood by my aunt that my siblings weren't afforded. Over the years, I was able to reconcile my memories as to why my life was enriched at that early age. I'm grateful to my late parents, who allowed a caring aunt to contribute to my upbringing. The gratitude I feel for my now adult siblings for loving me unconditionally over the years continues to make my life more fulfilling.

I enjoy the freedom to get into my car and drive anywhere my heart desires. The circumstance of being born in my country affords me freedoms many citizens of other countries don't experience. Had I not wanted to work after high school or college, I technically didn't *have to* find employment under the laws of my government. During an election cycle, I cast a vote for a candidate of my own choosing. At the present time, a large majority of people in my country are experiencing discontent with the elected leader and government administrators. It's very common to read comments on the internet filled with hate and slander regarding government officials on every level. The freedom to speak freely is being used now more than any time I can remember clearly. Assembly with like-minded individuals and participating in peaceful protests are other freedoms for which I'm grateful. I can marry and worship freely in my country, unlike many others around the world. My gratitude for the freedom to get an education and provide means for my child to become an educated adult is immense. The gratitude I feel is based on knowing my circumstances would be vastly different if I weren't born in a country that embraced democracy.

As an adult, I've known the joy and stress that comes with being a responsible member of society. Careers, relationships, and financial concerns of the past play a huge part in how I navigate through my life at the present time. It's not uncommon for me to observe family and friends on social media sites commenting on daily stresses regarding current news events, relationships, and their lives. I'm personally guilty of venting at times to my online social circle. Despite the unpleasant experiences at different times in my life, I've known true happiness. Knowing and feeling true happiness provides a reason to hope for better times. I believe most people want happiness in their jobs, personal relationships with loved ones, and physical health. Without past unpleasant experiences, I suspect there'd be no reason to be grateful. Why would gratitude be a part of our psyches if our lives were perfect? Knowing that times will get better keeps me hopeful and grateful to have my life. The stresses brought on by living in today's fast-paced world are cyclical in my experience. I'm always assured at some point, the circumstances will take a turn for the better.

Finally, the wealth of gratitude fueling my soul is given to my late parents and family members, who introduced the notion of a higher power to me at an early age. Witnessing evil, death, sickness, and heartache throughout my life would've been unbearable without the belief that a force unseen guides my life and causes me to be grateful.

# Thoughts on Racism in America from a Hopeful Human

As a United States citizen and a person of color, inequality, racism, police brutality, and the overall injustice faced by Black Americans are things I've been aware of since childhood. Seeing the injustices my family and other Blacks have faced remains a sad reality. For survival, one may have to learn peaceful coexistence with the hate caused by racism – but by no means acceptance. I imagine the aim for most is to live to see another day as we navigate through systemic racism in our country. It's evident through data and statistics[2] how racism is embedded in America's financial, legal, educational, employment, law enforcement, political, healthcare, housing, military, and many other areas. The current head of government in the United States has done little to unite the country or address racial discrimination.[3]

I grew up concurrently in a housing project and a working-class neighborhood with varying immigrant groups and nationalities. My elementary school had a small population of non-Blacks when I was in second grade. The number of non-Blacks in our neighborhood dwindled by the time I was in sixth grade. I can recall the number of non-Black families on one hand in my housing project before I was in middle school. On the other side of town, where I spent the summer and weekends with close relatives, I was exposed to interaction with other races well before I graduated from high school. At the time of my youth, most of my older relatives were born in the post-WWI era. Those relatives I speak of had experienced discrimination in America for all their lives. Their perseverance instructed survival to my generation. I watched my Black family and many others live their lives with devotion to God, hope, joy, and respect for their fellow man despite societal racism. The reality of racism was something I saw those around me in my early life navigate mostly with grace throughout their lives. Learning the history of enslaved Blacks in my country during my school years sparked my curiosity. As an elementary and middle school student, I took out library books on my own to read about Blacks who changed history. In high school, nothing would be more of an eye-opener on the experience of my ancestors than the *Roots* mini-series that aired on television for the first time. Before that, I had only read historical accounts of slavery in America geared toward school-age children. When I saw the graphic depiction of how African people, my ancestors, were enslaved and brought to America, my understanding of history was no longer abstract. The images I saw on my television had more of a visceral effect on me at the time than intellectual. I remember feeling uneasy as I sat in my integrated high school classrooms after the mini-series aired. I didn't know how my non-Black classmates felt about seeing *Roots* air on television, and I didn't ask. My Black friends had a lot to discuss with each other about the program. Still, I felt happy to have the non-Black friends who treated me with the same respect I gave them. I recall being allowed to go to certain amusement parks while avoiding others. My friends and I were told by our elders some places were 'for Whites' only.[4] Those elders experienced racism in their youth at those venues firsthand. Whether the White-only label given to those venues in my city was official or unspoken, my Black friends and I followed suit in avoiding those places. It wasn't until our Amusement park was no longer available that we ventured outside our comfort zones. I realize some of my Black friends had a different experience. I can only speak for my own experience at the time. I remember the same issues with public pools in the summer. My friends and I were forbidden to travel to certain neighborhoods in my city where our parents knew we wouldn't be welcome or safe. I can honestly say I didn't feel less of a person with the knowledge my race wasn't welcome in certain areas of my city. My parents raised me to be proud of my heritage and verbally told my siblings and me that we were equal with any man or woman, no matter the color. The lessons from my parents and older family mentors carried me throughout my life. As I met people of different races throughout my life, it was easier to communicate and form lasting relationships, knowing I felt like an equal citizen no matter if society hadn't caught up with what the Founding Fathers proposed in 1776.[5] Back then and to this very day, I'm frustrated when I'm reminded an individual sees my skin color as a flaw in my character or worth as a human being. The frustration quickly turns to pity for the ignorance I witnessed.

It wasn't until I worked in corporate America as a young adult that I felt I wasn't seen by some coworkers outside my race as I saw myself. I experienced being treated with respect and kindness by my direct management and coworkers of all races. The reality was that in more than one instance, I found a disparity in my compensation versus my non-Black coworkers with the same level of experience, work performance, and education. My conclusion was that the worth of the work I'd performed was considered less valuable than my peers. There were also many instances of myself, and other Black coworkers being excluded in events outside of work by presumed non-Black coworker friends. In my previous studies for a college degree, I recall a course in Sociology. The course content discussed how individuals in the workplace naturally gravitate and feel more comfortable with people who share similar backgrounds. The knowledge in the course made logical sense and gave me a better understanding of human behavior. The course gave me nothing to deal with the racism I'd face at that time and going forward in my life - as it wasn't the intent of the course. Growing up, seeing racism and stereotypical behavior on all sides became normal since it was my experience since birth. I admit that gaining an advanced education and life experience changed my views on race from when I was younger. I realize people still believe deep-seated stereotypes in our society. On an almost daily basis, I've read comments from online posts where people give stereotypical views that would blow your mind. My life experience with people of different races has caused me to view each person as an individual, not as a collective group based on race. My oldest grandchild is a teenager in the Generation Z category. She told me once in the past that she didn't think of color in her interactions with friends and classmates. She went on to say if a person is a jerk, they're a jerk no matter the color. For a while now, I've felt the younger generation is this nation and the world's greatest hope. In my journey as a God-fearing person, I treat my fellow human beings as I'd want to be treated. Sometimes that method of understanding doesn't work. With all that said, I'm blessed to have blood-related family and friends from a mixture of different races and ethnicities.

When I was growing up, I knew of only a few close older relatives who had served in WWII and Korea. Those military veterans seldom talked about their service to their country in my presence. It was a recent search of my family tree that revealed a couple of relatives who had military service I'd never known about. Those older relatives are gone from this world. I've often wondered how they felt to serve their country and, in turn, be treated less than equally both in the military and at home. I understand there are veterans today still experiencing the effects of systemic racism in the United States. It's difficult for me to imagine the feeling of risking one's life in service to a country and having your sacrifices and contributions to its success ignored. Around the age of twelve, I had the experience of being on the listening end of conversations with a veteran who frequented my relative's house. This man was a Black non-commissioned officer who served in WWII. For whatever reason, I was never asked to leave the room when he was present, as with other adult visitors. I grew up in an era where children didn't sit around what we called *'grown folks'* while they were talking. This veteran could talk for hours about his experiences as a Black soldier in World War II. A great deal of his language was graphic when he described his interaction with the non-Black officers and soldiers. He would discuss the racial epithets used toward him and his fellow Black soldiers. I recall this man discussing the all-Black unit he led as a sergeant. I listened as the man talked about trying to gain the respect of the men he led while having no authority over a White soldier of lesser rank – something his White counterparts didn't have to experience. I was intrigued and asked question after question as this man gave me what I now know was a valuable firsthand account of the experiences of a Black soldier in WWII. I regret not having the foresight or maturity to ask permission to use my tape cassette recorder during our conversations. In retrospect, I feel fortunate the man put up with the naïve questions I posed as he spoke of his war experiences. He was patient and answered all of my questions – some with brutal honesty that aged me a little when I heard the answers.

The recent tragedies of individuals losing their lives because of racism, police brutality, and social injustice have sparked protests across my country and even the world. Those horrific situations that led to the recent protests and looting are still in the news as I pen this piece. The most encouraging thing about the public outcry is seeing people of all races, ages, and backgrounds come together to protest the social plague affecting our country. There are many of the younger generations from all races who might not have experienced racism, disparate treatment, or social injustice in their lives to this point. However, those young people of all colors stand on the front lines of protest just the same. In the wake of what seems like a barrage of police brutality and racial/social injustice, I'm encouraged. The recent peaceful protests and initial policy changes of individual state governments have started to promote healing and change. These protests need not get lost over time. As Americans, we need to remember and speak the names of the people whose lives were snuffed out by police brutality, racism, and outdated policing policies. We need to speak their names until disenfranchised people of color, sexual orientation, and all others get the same justice and opportunities as every other American. We know the names. We've seen the news reports' graphic videos. I believe we'll continue to read their stories. Unfortunately, more injustices will be revealed in the future, as recent history has shown.

My hope is that decent and concerned Americans strive to shine a light on racism and social injustice in our country until the non-believers understand the existence of both. As an American citizen, you can make a difference. Whether you're physically able to march in protest or join activism efforts online, by telephone, or in your community, we must keep our voices loud. Many are calling this history in America today a *watershed* moment. Let's move forth and not rest in our efforts for equality in America. Until we come together as a nation on one accord, we won't achieve the promise of Lincoln's Gettysburg Address that "all men are created equal."[6]

# Being a Better Human – What's so Difficult?

There's another name added to the countless Black men and women's lives lost due to police brutality in the United States. Tyre Nichols, a Black man, was the latest victim at the hands of those sworn to protect and serve the community. Mr. Nichols died of injuries on January 10, 2023 – three days after receiving a brutal beating by Memphis police officers at an apparent traffic stop on January 7, 2023. There are plenty of details available online for anyone curious about all the horrific details. A tragic video exists that documents the savage way this 29-year-old man received injuries, resulting in his death. At this time, in early February 2023, five police officers were already charged in connection with Tyre Nichols's murder. There are multiple counts, including aggravated kidnapping, second-degree murder, aggravated assault, official misconduct, and official suppression – according to televised reports from January 26, 2023.

Thoughts are prayers by sincere people do matter but don't do much to help the heartbreak of the mothers, fathers, and families of the victims of unnecessary violence by law enforcement. It doesn't have to be said, but common sense lets us know all policemen aren't the same. But this piece isn't about the good law enforcement men and women who execute their jobs with fairness and dignity to their public. What's being discussed in this case is the police officers who fail to honor their oath to protect the public they serve. Reports of Tyre Nichols's mother attempting to watch the video of his beating are unimaginable to me as a parent. RowVaughn Wells, Tyre Nichols's mother, was said to have watched the video for less than a minute.[7] No parent should have to bury their child – a phrase that we've all heard too much in recent years.

Aside from the obvious outcry that widespread law enforcement reform is needed in America, significant legislation has yet to pass. The George Floyd Policing Act of 2020 was passed by the Democrats in the House of Representatives in 2021. Unfortunately, efforts to pass it in the Senate were unsuccessful.

In this instance, justice was swift for the perpetrators of another unjust crime against a Black person by law enforcement. A mere ten days after Mr. Nichols's death, police officers were fired by their Memphis police department. In addition, reports today indicate another police officer was fired, and two first responders were suspended in connection with Tyre Nichols's death.[8] Does it matter that, in this particular case, the officers were Black and menacing a Black citizen? Some would say the swift justice brought against the officers had plenty to do with the race of the officers. Who knows – not I. There's something lacking in America's system of justice.

A larger issue, in my opinion, is the lack of humanity of people, in general, at this time in history. Whether or not the officers were taught proper arrest techniques, this devastating tragedy shouldn't have happened. Where was the understanding and consideration of human life by these officers and those in past cases of police brutality? Watching the video, I saw no pause or mercy, compassion, from the five officers who committed the heinous act against Tyre Nichols. This wasn't the first video on record showing police brutality. However, it was the most gut-wrenching I'd ever watched from the countless other videos of police brutality that exist. No human being should be treated by their fellow man like Tyre Nichols and the countless others who suffered at the hands of those who held the public's trust. For me, watching the video was necessary. Burying our heads in the sand as Americans and hoping for a change is worthless.

Shouldn't human beings, especially those placed in authority, strive to be better humans? No matter what instruction or lack of education is gained by our jobs, empathy matters – common sense matters. Yes, updated police reform laws are in desperate need in the United States. But where is the love for another living person? Training alone can't effectively teach love and compassion for one's fellow man. Empathy must be inherent in one's character – to some extent, in my opinion. All human beings deserve the respect of being allowed to live to face any possible charges or crimes in a court of law. At least, that's what we're taught at an early age in school and by most of our families about living in a democratic society.

# Perspective

How we feel about a subject or something happening in our lives can be in stark contrast to someone else's beliefs. Whenever the topic of why things are perceived differently from one person to the next arises, perspective can be the root cause of those feelings.

Perspective can be a difficult thing to understand at times. In matters of personal connections, for example, it's possible to die on a hill of misunderstanding. Expectations and misconceptions can cause havoc in our relationships.

A person can live confident in their failures and triumphs. Another individual's perspective of those same failures and triumphs can often differ. The facts of the issue may be somewhere in the middle of both parties' viewpoints. The indisputable reality may be that there is no credible way to walk the same path as another and still have the same perspective. Feelings, experiences, and understanding are often not equal for two different mindsets. The ability to see another's side of an issue can get complicated in various situations. A neutral party can sometimes evaluate the incident to decipher facts. When an impartial party gives its viewpoint, existing misconceptions are illuminated.

A profound thing I've found regarding perspective is how people can shield themselves from past trauma. Trauma can transform our minds to accept a false narrative where reality is distorted – I've seen this in real life. Think about the differences between *Gen X and Baby Boomer* generation's perspectives on childhood trauma. My opinion on this subject is purely speculation based on things I've heard from both groups. Baby Boomers may categorize the feeling of not being "seen" by their parents as the person they were inside. Some Boomers respond with "that's the way things were" or "it was what it was." While some Gen Xers feel they may need ongoing therapy for the trauma they experienced in childhood, such as feeling abandoned as a *latch-key* child.[9] Who's to say which generation is wrong or right? Our sole perspectives dictate our reactions to most things in our lives. Until further understanding of our true selves or a given subject happens – our perspectives will stay the same.

# POETRY & PROSE

# Never

Never, no doubt, spans to infinity. In my youth, I enjoyed the naiveté of stating what I would or wouldn't do. I'd defy anyone who'd challenge me on what I deemed convictions.

Life has a great way of squashing any wisdom about oneself you'd thought accurate. As we experience inner growth over time, we often find the never we so boldly preached sometimes becomes a maybe or reality.

You see, my belief is that knowing yourself is absolute for a finite moment in time. Next year, or better yet tomorrow, can bring with it doubts. Fate often steps in to test your resolve. Never can teach life lessons.

When you make the mistake of assigning the never to someone other than yourself, you revel in ignorance. The human psyche and its complications are unlimited. Make the mistake of labeling a never to another and find out.

I found, after years of life lessons, how romanticizing the word never narrowed my purview. I continue to grasp the concept of allowing for possibilities beyond my observations. Life has taught me never to say never.

## Hello, Juneteenth!

Your introduction to the masses is bittersweet.

Yet, I welcome the national recognition and

illumination of a glorious day in Black history.

You're familiar to some and unfamiliar to others.

Our country will now spotlight your importance by

acknowledging you're worthy of being remembered.

The nation seems to be moving toward

necessary change for the equitable treatment of all

citizens. The tragic past can serve as a lesson for the future.

I can imagine our enslaved ancestors' expectations of living a life of impartiality after the War Between the States was over.

You're official, and I can cautiously say that hope is on my horizon. You are no longer a footnote on the pages of history.

Legislation marking a day of freedom for the last of this nation's enslaved people is fine and good. The work of that freedom proposed so long ago remains in progress.

The dream of my people's promised equality will remain unrealized in my lifetime. My grandchildren may live to experience the fruits of their ancestors' labors.

Today, I embrace the small victories won by past heroes in the fight for Black people's equality. The smell of healing is in the air. We must not linger in our efforts.

But the struggle for true equality and all it entails is real.

Recognition of a past marred with inhumanity is a

great move forward. We make you official, Juneteenth.

Our nation honors its independence on July $4^{th}$.

Juneteenth, I believe the ancestors see you and give the nod.

I celebrate you and continue to hope.

# Forever Blue

The elusiveness kept me guessing

and happily mesmerized.


That they're no longer in my presence

Sends me to the depths of sadness.


I walk on familiar and favorite streets

to stop and reminisce.


I keep my smiles captive now since a

A worthy substitute is yet to be found.


Leave me to my blues and sprits until

I no longer feel the pain.

# Love

I truly believe that what we humans call LOVE in its purest form transcends all living species. When I see love shown by human beings to their children or loved ones unconditionally and, in turn, see how a simple creature can show love by protecting its offspring - I know that LOVE must be a gift from God to the universe.

# QUOTES

"Rejoice in the harsh lessons life teaches you as they have made you the spectacular person you are at this moment in time."

©2002 R. H. Wallace

"Life is hard enough without trying to fit into boxes created by other people. Embrace your authentic self and break free."

©2019 R. H. W. Dorsey

"Live well, leaving no victims and causing little harm while speaking your truth. You'll have no regrets."

©2022 R. H. W. Dorsey

"Losing a loved one can be a devastating event in your life. It's possible never to feel the same love again. Life provides you a silver lining of knowing that type of love existed."

©2024 R. H. W. Dorsey

"I truly believe that what we humans call LOVE in its purest form transcends all living species. When I see love shown by human beings to their children or loved ones unconditionally, and in turn see how a simple creature can show love by protecting its offspring - I know that LOVE must be a gift from God to the universe."

©2010 R. H. W. Dorsey

"When you decide to live your life despite what's supposed to happen or might happen, you move forward."

©2011 R.H.W. Dorsey

"Life is teaching you even when you're not aware you're learning."

©2002 R.H.W. Dorsey

# ESSAY

# Justification

When a person starts explaining away questionable or immoral behavior, it's easy to notice rationalizing at work. Years ago, someone I considered wise told me, *"When you start to rationalize, be careful. You may be on the road to ruin."* The advice turned out to be valuable in future unconfident situations.

As flawed humans, we may, at times, justify our own evil or immoral behavior by rationalizing. We convince ourselves that there is a good reason for our actions by using the justification as self-preservation. Have you ever talked yourself into feeling better after you've done something you have since regretted because of an undesired outcome? Lying to ourselves is a fantastic way to rid the guilty conscience. However, we don't call the rationalizing we do as 'lying.'

People often downplay the severity of their actions regarding their friends or loved ones. We justify those people by using a variety of excuses to explain their behavior. It's human nature to support the special people in our lives in good and bad times. Should we sacrifice our convictions to support those we care about? It's an individual decision.

I've witnessed constituents set aside their principles to justify the despicable actions of their political office choices. I often wonder about those who follow a candidate with blind devotion. A couple of questions that enter my mind in this scenario: Is the outcome of an election worth sacrificing your moral compass? Do the actions of your political candidate mirror your actual values? Will you, as a voter, feign outrage when your candidate does something that seems to have been foreseeable?

Eventually, as we grow up and go about our daily lives, justification will somehow be involved in our actions.

# On Miracles

I have sometimes wondered what people think when they hear the word miracle. I am speaking of miracles related to events in the world that defy scientific evidence. This brief essay intends to address the subject of medical miracles. The Merriam-Webster dictionary defines the word miracle as: *"An extraordinary event manifesting divine intervention in human affairs."* It is logical to conclude that people worldwide have varying interpretations of what constitutes a miracle. An individual's belief system evaluates the mysteries that go against rules in the natural environment. Persons with contrasting religious ideologies may view one event differently than someone with beliefs other than their own. Medical miracles are believed to have occurred when an outcome is optimistic despite the overwhelming evidence that a dire conclusion would be met. Analytical people, including the medical staff, may view a situation with this reasoning: *"Well, we are glad things turned out the way they did. As much as we know about the human body, there is still much to learn.* In those cases, the significance of what some would call a 'miraculous' event is downplayed. Subsequent explanations by the experts for these medical miracles can involve a technical breakdown of why the educated guesses became invalid in that situation. Outliers can exist, correct?

As a student of life, I believe some things in this world are beyond human understanding. My personal belief from childhood remains that there is a higher power guiding our lives and directing events in the universe - God.

Of course, not everyone believes there is an omnipotent source that controls our existence. Many labels categorize people's beliefs or non-beliefs in a deity. In most societies, peaceful coexistence with others' beliefs is a part of daily life. Mutual respect for faiths other than ours allows us to live in harmony—until it does not. How does one who does not believe in a deity reconcile things that defy scientific evidence? I cannot answer that question.

On the issue of miracles, the following is a situation I witnessed. An eighty-seven-year-old female in poor health was admitted to a hospital during a skilled nursing stay at a nursing home in the Spring of the year 2020. The woman's admission to the hospital was for complications of the COVID-19 virus. During that time, medical professionals were still learning about the virus that would eventually prove deadly for millions of people around the world. Before contracting the virus, this older woman was receiving medications for atrial fibrillation issues, asthma, COPD, degenerative arthritis, and end-stage renal disease. She was a dialysis patient. The COVID-19 virus compromised the woman's lungs enough to get her admitted to a hospital's intensive care unit. The consensus by a majority of the medical team following her case was that she had only a slight chance of surviving since the virus had weakened her entire respiratory system. The woman became bedridden while in the inpatient hospital facility. This patient's Living Will specified that she did not choose to be put on a ventilator if the need arose with a deteriorating medical status. The family representative was also the woman's caregiver before the nursing home confinement. At one point in the critical hospital stay, the family was notified of the grave news of the woman's declining vitals. The medical staff monitoring the woman's care concluded their patient would not survive the deadly virus that continued to spread across continents during that time. The overall message to the patient's family was that it was time to say goodbye to their loved one as soon as possible.

The family was informed of the facility's policy of restricting visitors for COVID-19 patients. A concerned social worker made an exception for one or two family members on that day. Three family members traveled over fifty miles to the hospital to see their loved one, possibly for the last time. Upon arrival at the hospital, the doctor and social worker explained there was a turn of events in the woman's medical condition. The woman's medical status had improved in the prior ninety minutes. The conversation between one of the family members and the woman who lay in the intensive care unit included prayers of healing and strength. The medical professionals were cautious in their projection that the woman would ultimately overcome the illness. There were overwhelming statistics of similar confinements that ended in the patient expiring.

The older adult survived the acute care and continued to rehabilitate with skilled care at the nursing home. There were a couple of short-lived hospital stays after the women's discharge from the hospital in the months that followed the COVID-19 inpatient stay. Still, the woman's condition improved, and she could walk again. The older woman became well enough to return home to live with her family caregivers. I truly believe this woman's survival was the product of a miracle.

Did God answer all the family, friends, and loved ones' prayers on behalf of the woman? Did a miracle happen, or just a strong will to survive on the patient's part? Was medical intervention the only reason the woman survived? We decide for ourselves.

# On Grief

I recently read one definition of the word *grief*. The Merriam-Webster dictionary defines *grief* as: "deep and poignant distress caused by or as if by bereavement. Years ago, I learned that grief could manifest in many ways depending on the individual's perspective. As unique beings, our definitions of the word grief can be varied. What follows explores this author's view on grief related to bereavement.

In my experience, grief can sometimes present itself when a person least expects it. The feeling of deep sorrow comes and goes from our psyche as time passes—like a never-ending spiral. I believe the grief that leaves us is not entirely gone but in hibernation. I believe that the human mind is sometimes given a grace period to survive a tragedy of loss. That is to say; our minds do not succumb to sadness to the point where we cannot move on with our lives.

The first funeral I can remember attending as a young child left me with questions. My curious nature caused me to wonder what reaction I needed to express at the ceremony. In my brief experience at that early age, seeing the unique responses to the sad event confused me. The authority figures in my life were dealing with grief at that moment in various ways from what my minimal experience with life would expect at the time. I saw an older adult cry for the first time that day – which turned out to be the last time I would witness it in that person. Another influential adult in my life seemed unfeeling on that day –a stark contrast to what I knew of that person. The facial expressions, including out-of-character behaviors from most present at the funeral, seemed like a weird dream.

Life, time, and maturity have taught me the individuality and personal nature of grief. Everyone who has loved or cared for someone other than themselves is subject to grief. The process we work through within ourselves concerning grief is necessary for spiritual healing. It's the nature of some to expect a person to behave in a certain way when grieving. Have you ever judged how someone should've conducted themselves during their grief? If we're being honest with ourselves, most of us have been on the side of judging others at one time or another. But does grief have a blueprint? Our society has rituals and norms that most of us follow in times of grief. However, the individual's response to a tragedy may be a cumulation of life experience, their relationship with the deceased, and many other factors. Knowing another's life story and personal experience is impossible for most. However, as imperfect humans, we judge. I've witnessed people attend funerals displaying deep emotions for a deceased person for whom they barely showed interest in life. Who am I to judge their reasons or behavior? Some people smile and appear happy in public when their insides are raging with sadness. Other people show their distress with ease around large groups of people. The bottom line is that no one should dictate how another manages their grief, except in cases where a person is showing behavior that's harmful to themselves.

The impact someone has on our lives is not always apparent until they are no longer on this earth. It often takes an absence for some to appreciate the influence another had in their life. We've all heard that *time is a great healer*, correct? I believe healing from a loss involves time and reflection at one's own pace. If the feelings of grief are not addressed constructively, it's likely an inevitable guess that a flare-up of emotions will happen at some point in the future. I believe we, as individuals, are stronger than we imagine ourselves to be at times. I've seen people experience an unthinkable tragedy, and many agreed that the person affected would have their spirit broken. Instead, for some, a tragic event may test their resolve without causing a mental breakdown, for instance.

Grief is inevitable if we've ever felt love for family, friends, and romantic relationships. When those associations end due to death, most people grieve. The process of grieving, in my opinion, can be a gift of sorts. Why can grief be a gift? I believe if you've truly loved someone, grieving is essential and, most times, unavoidable. Grief allows us to remember and hold our loved ones in our hearts and memories. Love is a gift, and grieving will eventually be a part of the process for those of us who survive our loved ones.

# POETRY & PROSE

# Apathy Siege

An endless siege of apathy spreads

like wildfires as we ignore hunger

and human suffering.

We side-eye the needy as a

Passing nuisance.

To seek the solution within

ourselves, we must awaken

our senses.

## You Chose Violence

On a sunny day full of promise and joy for the

plans we made; you chose violence. My heart

was ripped into shreds and then transformed

into necessary apathy to survive the siege of

misery that would follow me into dark corners of

my mind and haunt my day and night dreams.


You chose the violence of ghosting the one that

poured kindness and love into your life. An explanation

of your absence would've been merciful. A mere note

with an offer to kiss where the sun doesn't shine

would've been welcome. I now realize the closure I seek

will never be mine. You're alive and well and painting the town.

As I watched you pass me on the street, you're as a stranger. I caught your eye for an instant and noticed the trajectory of your own eyes fall to the ground like acid rain on the pavement. I choose to believe the guilt of your betrayal has haunted your soul on some level. Your act of violence didn't bruise my body, but fractured my pride. The mark left on my heart is steadily disappearing as I journey on the road to healing.

I'm now fueled with purpose as I embrace self-love and care for a precious soul that I should've guarded against the likes of a violence maker such as you. That we didn't work out isn't the thing - I can accept a wrong decision. But, to end us on a high note, and with absolute silence is cruel. You chose violence.

# Hate Exists

Hate exists among itself

and has no redeeming qualities.

Evil lives in the most surprising

places.

The unrecognizable villain masquerades

throughout our lives from birth to death.

If we're fortunate, our existence isn't

well-scathed with the scars of hate to guide

us through our journey to forever.

# QUOTES

"Using the past as blame for your current situation does little to propel you forward – release the mental chains that hold you back."

©2024 R. H. W. Dorsey

"Contemplate the wisdom of someone who has walked a path you plan to explore."

©2024 R. H. W. Dorsey

"Demonstrate your known capabilities to invalidate opinions by others who doubt your abilities."

©2024 R. H. W. Dorsey

"A good friend won't stay silent when you're in need, even if all they can offer is moral support."

©2024 R. H. W. Dorsey

"Losing a loved one can be a devastating event in your life. It's possible never to feel the same love again. Life provides you a silver lining in knowing that type of love existed."

©2024 R. H. W. Dorsey

# End Notes

[1] https://fountainmagazine.com/about/the-fountain-essay-contest-2018-shortlist

[2] https://onlinelibrary.wiley.com/doi/full/10.1111/1475-6773.13220.

[3] https://www.politico.com/story/2018/05/08/trump-obama-racial-bias-522940.

[4] https://2020census.gov/en/about-questions/2020-census-questions-race.html.

[5] https://www.ushistory.org/declaration/document/.

[6] http://www.abrahamlincolnonline.org/lincoln/speeches/gettysburg.htm.

[7] https://www.washingtonpost.com/nation/2023/01/27/tyre-nichols-family-police-beating-video/.

[8] https://www.cnn.com/2023/02/03/us/tyre-nichols-memphis-investigation-district-attorney/index.html.

[9] "Latchkey child." Merriam-Webster.com Dictionary, Merriam-Webster, https://www.merriam-webster.com/dictionary/latchkey%20child. Accessed 31 May. 2024.

www.ingramcontent.com/pod-product-compliance
Lightning Source LLC
La Vergne TN
LVHW012037060526
838201LV00061B/4644